The Golden Horde: The History and Legacy of the Mongol Khanate

By Charles River Editors

A medieval depiction of the Battle of Mohi

About Charles River Editors

Charles River Editors is a boutique digital publishing company, specializing in bringing history back to life with educational and engaging books on a wide range of topics. Keep up to date with our new and free offerings with [this 5 second sign up on our weekly mailing list](), and visit [Our Kindle Author Page]() to see other recently published Kindle titles.

We make these books for you and always want to know our readers' opinions, so we encourage you to leave reviews and look forward to publishing new and exciting titles each week.

Introduction

A medieval depiction of Batu Khan establishing the Golden Horde

In a world fascinated by men like Alexander the Great and Julius Caesar, Genghis Khan is one of history's greatest and most famous conquerors. No man, before or since, has ever started with so little and gone on to achieve so much. From a noble family but raised in poverty that drove him to the brink of starvation, Genghis Khan rose to control the second-largest empire the world has ever known (the largest being, arguably, the British Empire of the 18th and 19th centuries), and easily the largest empire conquered by a single man. And while many empires disintegrate upon the death of an emperor, like Alexander the Great's, Genghis Khan's empire endured and was actually enlarged by his successors, who went on to establish dynasties that in some cases lasted for centuries.

Though history is usually written by the victors, the lack of a particularly strong writing tradition from the Mongols ensured that history was largely written by those who they vanquished. Because of this, their portrayal in the West and the Middle East has been extraordinarily (and in many ways unfairly) negative for centuries, at least until recent revisions to the historical record. The Mongols have long been depicted as wild horse-archers galloping out of the dawn to rape, pillage, murder and enslave, but the Mongol army was a highly sophisticated, minutely organized and incredibly adaptive and innovative institution, as witnessed by the fact that it was successful in conquering enemies who employed completely different weaponry and different styles of fighting, from Chinese armored infantry to Middle Eastern camel cavalry and Western knights and men-at-arms. Likewise, the infrastructure and administrative corps which governed the empire, though largely borrowed from the Chinese, was inventive, practical, and extraordinarily modern and efficient. This was no fly-by-night enterprise but a sophisticated, complex, and extremely well-oiled machine.

While the Golden Horde technically refers to part of the Mongol Empire, today the Golden Horde is often used interchangeably with the Mongol forces as a whole. As such, the Golden Horde conjures vivid images of savage, barbarian horsemen riding across the steppes, an unstoppable force mindlessly slaughtering and burning. It is often imagined that they conquered by sheer brutality and terror, and that they epitomized everything that came from the east: uncivilized, brutal and undisciplined.

This sensationalized image, impressed upon the West by Hollywood and by the perception of the "Yellow Peril" that has colored Western views toward Asia for a long time, began almost from the beginning. The Mongols treasured art and literature and protected religion, that of their subjects as well as their own, and trade, commerce, and cultural exchanges flourished under the Golden Horde and the other Mongol khanates, but that escaped the notice of their contemporaries. Giovanni de Plano Carpini, a papal envoy journeying through Russia on his way to the Khan of the Golden Horde, noted, "They [the Mongols] attacked Rus', where they made great havoc, destroying cities and fortresses and slaughtering men; and they laid siege to Kiev, the capital of Rus'; after they had besieged the city for a long time, they took it and put the inhabitants to death. When we were journeying through that land we came across countless skulls and bones of dead men lying about on the ground. Kiev had been a very large and thickly populated town, but now it has been reduced almost to nothing, for there are at the present time scarce two hundred houses there and the inhabitants are kept in complete slavery."[1]

What can't be disputed is that the Golden Horde directly affected Eastern Europe for nearly 250 years, and even after its rapid rise brought about a long, tortuous decline, it has continued to shape the destiny of that region. *The Golden Horde: The History and Legacy of the Mongol Khanate* examines the events that led to the rise of the khanate, what life was like there, and how the Mongols fought. Along with pictures depicting important people, places, and events, you will learn about the Golden Horde like never before.

---

[1] "The Destruction of Kiev". Tspace.library.utoronto.ca. Archived from the original on 19 August 2016.

The Golden Horde: The History and Legacy of the Mongol Khanate

About Charles River Editors

Introduction

    Uniting the Mongols

    The Origins of the Golden Horde

    The Golden Horde's Government and Society

    The Horde Under Uzbeg

    The Decline of the Horde

    The Legacy of the Golden Horde

    Online Resources

    Further Reading

Free Books by Charles River Editors

Discounted Books by Charles River Editors

Uniting the Mongols

One of the most amazing aspects of the empire Genghis Khan would conquer and consolidate is its humble origins. History's great conquerors have, by and large, had the advantage of a leg up in kick-starting their careers. Alexander the Great inherited an almost pitch-perfect military machine from his father, the great reformer of the Macedonian army. Julius Caesar had the benefit of a centuries-old warrior society dedicated to conquest and expansion at his back. Napoleon could call upon the resources of a state which, though impoverished and recently revolutionized, was still one of the oldest and most powerful in Europe. Genghis Khan had none of this. His starting point was a loosely scattered collection of warrior nomad tribes, some organized into federations, all fiercely independent, and almost all hostile to all outsiders. It would require strong will and genius to forge these steppe warriors into one of history's greatest fighting forces.

Hard places breed hard men, and the steppes of Mongolia, where Genghis Khan was born, are such a place. The "sea of grass" was populated by the Mongols, fiercely independent tribal nomads who wondered from place to place in search of forage and food. They were renowned archers and horsemen, and the horse was revered in Mongolian culture as a central part of an individual's existence; horses provided transportation in a land where distances were colossal and food in the form of dried horseflesh, fermented mare's milk and milk curds, all staples of the Mongolian diet. Their way of life was simple, that of hunter-gatherers and tribal warriors, and even their prayers, which revolved around worship of the sky, seem crude today.

The Mongols were inured to extraordinary hardship and were reputed to be able to endure days on end in the saddle, subsisting solely on scraps of food and blood from their own horses, which were just as tough as themselves, if not tougher. Soft life was despised in Mongolia as being both effeminate and beyond contemplation, and those who practiced it (i.e. other cultures) were regarded as effeminate and weak. It was into this harsh land that Genghis Khan was born, sometime between 1160 and 1170 A.D., not far from the modern Mongolian capital of Ulaan-Bataar. Sources for his early life are fragmentary and uncertain because it was only when Genghis Khan came into contact with cultures with a strong written tradition that his historical narrative became more authoritative, but historians have been able to piece together much of his childhood and early achievements with reasonable accuracy.

The Onon River in Mongolia, the region where Genghis Khan was born and grew up

Genghis Khan was born with the name Temujin at birth, the son of Yesugei Khan of the Borjigin tribe and Holeun of the Olkhunut, and he was apparently named after a Tatar warlord that Yesugei had defeated in battle. He was Yesugei's third son (his first with Holeun), with two older brothers named Hasar and Haciun, and he was later joined by a younger brother named Temuge. He also had a sister, Temulen, and two half-brothers, Behter and Belgutei. There is no reliable record of what Temujin actually looked like, as most of the portraits of him that survive were produced after his lifetime and accounts describing him are in all likelihood fraught with symbolism and represent popular and prophetic conceptions of a foreign conqueror more than Temujin's actual appearance. One of the most authoritative and comprehensive descriptions of his appearance comes from the Persian historian Rashid-ad-Din, who somewhat incongruously describes him as being tall in stature with red hair and green eyes. Those were not the physical attributes of a typical Mongol at the time, but it is possible Temujin possessed these physical characteristics since they do occur among Mongolian people to this day.

Several portents are said to have surrounded his birth, though these are most likely largely apocryphal. The most popular one claims that Temujin emerged from Holeun's womb with a blood clot clutched in his fist, an ancient omen which signified he would grow to become a ruler. However, this fate was not immediately apparent because when Temujin was around six years old, his mother Holeun gave birth to another boy, Temuge. According to Mongol tradition it was

Temuge who would inherit the larger portion of Yesugei's wealth and his title, as the youngest son of a ruler traditionally inherited. This system, of course, is in stark contrast with the Western world's more familiar custom of having the eldest son inherit.

Despite the fact that Yesugei apparently did not intend for Temujin to be his successor, he did not intend to leave him penniless either, and a fitting match was arranged for him at a very young age as was common among the Mongols. When Temujin was just nine he was sent by his father to the nearby Onggirat tribe, where he was taken in by the family of Borte, a girl who was to be his future wife. As was customary, her family looked after his upbringing until he reached the age of 12, when it was expected he would marry. Once they did marry, Borte would bring Temujin a sizeable dowry in return for the honor of being married to a Khan's son, but until then Temujin was expected to serve Borte's family.

Much of his education had already taken place at this point, for he would be considered a man at 12, and at that age Temujin was already a proficient rider, wrestler, archer and hunter. As fate would have it, these skills would be of crucial importance to his family and himself in the following years because, unbeknownst to him as he watched his father ride away, the first crisis of a life full of them was approaching.

On his way back from delivering Temujin to the Onggirat, Yesugei met a party of travelling Tatars, his erstwhile enemies, and he agreed to eat with them. During the encounter, however, the Tatars poisoned him, and Yesugei died shortly thereafter. When news of this reached Temujin, he immediately left the Onggirat and hurried home, where he presented himself before the Borjigin and announced he would take Yesugei's place as Khan. Not surprisingly, the young teen was scorned by the Borjigin, who reckoned he was too young and untested to fill Yesugei's shoes. In a cruel but not uncommon turn of events, he, his mother, his brothers, his sister and his half-brothers were abandoned by the Borjigin, left to fend for themselves with virtually nothing but the clothes on their backs during a winter on the steppes without horses or the support of a tribe.

This rapid turn of events was made all the more devastating by the fact that the tribal system meant a Mongol's tribe was everything to him. Without it, he was an outcast, a nothing, in danger not merely of starvation on the unforgiving sea of grass but also of consequence-free enslavement or killing. Temujin endured this life for years, barely scraping by as an outcast with the constant threat of starvation always staring him in the face, and it was during this time that his mother drummed one of the lessons that would come to dominate Temujin's future policies into him: the tribe was all, and alliances were vital to escape the outcast's life. Holeun and her children survived on scraps, the leavings of other tribes, and what they could hunt, dressing themselves in animal skins and living in shelters they built themselves. While these were obvious hardships, it was during this difficult time that Temujin's natural resourcefulness and inclination to leadership led him to become the virtual head of the household, a position for which he competed with his elder half-brothers Behter and Belgutei, who resented him as an upstart. Temujin, however, was made of stronger stuff than they, and he proved that even as a pre-teen he was old and ruthless beyond his years when he killed Behter after the older boy had refused to hand over the animals he had hunted for the common pot. And despite their position as outcasts, it appears as though even the small happenings of Temujin's renegade family still attracted attention among the Mongol tribes, for this killing seems to have been noticed, and it formed the first tassel of what was to be a fearsome reputation.

In 1182 Temujin and his family's solitary existence was rudely shattered when the Tayichiud, a local tribe who shared bonds of ancestry with the Borjigin and had been allies of Yesugei, seized Temujin in a raid and made him a slave. Temujin was forced to endure hardships even greater than those he had struggled through as an outcast, spending most of his days in a portable stock similar to an ox's yoke. In fact, his predicament was apparently so dire that one of his guards became sympathetic enough to his plight to help him escape the Taychiud. Temujin fled from captivity into the night and hid underneath a riverbank before managing to discard his yoke. This became yet another crucial part of is reputation, and his daring escape from the Taychiud led him to acquire a significant measure of notoriety on the plains, where such piratical acts were held in high regard.

Shortly after his escape Temujin met Jelme and Borchu, two warriors who agreed to enter his service and support his claim as Khan of the Borjigin. He was also joined by Jamukha, a young Mongol nobleman who was the son of his tribe's Khan, around this time, and Jamukha eventually became Temujin's blood-brother and closest friend. With renewed confidence following his growing status, Temujin presented himself to the Onggirat at age 16, demanding that Borte's father honour the agreement he had made to Yesugei and give him Borte's hand in marriage, something which the older man was honourable enough – or far-seeing enough – to do. Despite the fact that their marriage had been arranged, Temujin seems to have been truly in love with Borte, who was his one queen for life; though he did take lesser wives, as was expected of him, he never allowed any to replace Borte.

Shortly after his marriage, Temujin and his followers swore service to Toghrul Khan, Khan of the Kerait, a mighty confederation of Mongol tribes. Toghrul had been Yesugei's blood-brother, and it was because of that bond, and the young man's growing reputation, that he took Temujin's vow.

A medieval depiction of Genghis Khan and Toghrul Khan

Temujin would not regret taking the vow, because shortly afterwards Borte was kidnapped by the Merkits, a rival federation, and given as wife to one of their warriors. Temujin was distraught, but Toghrul Khan reportedly gave him 200,000 (almost certainly an inflated number) of his warriors and sent him to destroy the Merkits and, in so doing, get Borte back. Toghrul evidently recognized Temujin was a natural leader, and he took him under his wing and also encouraged Temujin to get help from his blood-brother Jamukha, who had risen to become Khan of the powerful Jadaran tribe while Temujin and Borte had been enjoying their married life.

The campaign – Temujin's first major war – was brief, bloody and extraordinarily successful. The Merkits were virtually annihilated in a series of battles and Temujin was able to recapture Borte unharmed, though not, if rumor is to be believed, untouched. Borte's first son, Jochi, was inconveniently born nine months after her ordeal, and though she and Temujin steadfastly refused to deny his parentage, doubt dogged him all through his life. At the same time, the campaign against the Merkits also marked the beginning of a falling-out with Jamukha despite their earlier bond of blood-brotherhood, and the rift would develop into an ever-greater rivalry.

In addition to getting his wife back, the victorious campaign against the Merkits brought Temujin vast amounts of power, prestige, and followers, and he began to be regarded as a serious warlord in his own right. With Toghrul's blessing, Temujin embarked upon a campaign in the following years to unify the tribes of central Mongolia under his own command. The tribes of the area, unlike the vast federations to the east and west, were largely disunited, allowing Temujin to swallow them up piecemeal despite the fact they were brave fighters. Temujin proved adept at playing the alliance game as well, persuading some tribes to yield bloodlessly to him and pitting some tribes against each other.

Temjuin also implemented policies that were nothing short of revolutionary. Traditionally, defeated tribes could look forward to a future of enslavement, summary execution or diaspora, but Temujin, possibly because he had been an outcast and slave himself, instead incorporated the vanquished into his own tribe, even going so far as having his mother Holeun adopt war orphans as her own in order to make children of the defeated tribe his half-brothers. This generous, humane approach won Temujin the appreciation and love of people who would otherwise revile him, and when defeated warriors realized that he would take them under his wing and grant them a share in the future spoils of victory, they flocked willingly to his banner. The institution of a system of promotion and rank within Temujin's fledgling army that was based not on blood and family but upon merit alone also meant that Temujin's generals and captains were among the very best the Mongols could produce, for they made their reputations and maintained them by the sword alone.

By 1190 Temujin had succeeded in bringing the entire region of central Mongolia under his direct control, forging its disparate, quarrelsome tribes into a single administrative and military entity. He was also a father at least three times over, as his wife had given birth to sons Chagatai, Ogadai and Tolui in the interim. It is unclear if other children died in infancy, or how many daughters he had if any, a clear indication that daughters were less important to chroniclers than sons.

Temujin's success did not go unnoticed, and it began to worry Toghrul, who still believed Temujin would stay faithful to him despite the fact he was blossoming into a powerful warlord who used "radical" policies that made his subjects far more loyal to him than usual. Toghrul's apprehension was exacerbated by his jealous son Sengum, who was bitterly resentful of Temujin. Sengum felt temujin was usurping his place in his father's affections, and he wasted no time in pouring poison into Toghrul's ear, warning him that Temujin would soon be powerful enough to depose him. Sengum suggested that his father should rid himself of Temujin right away, and it appears Sengum and his faction made an attempt on Temujin's life around this time. The attempt almost certainly occurred with Toghrul's tacit consent, and Temujin certainly suspected as much, for the relationship between the two, which had previously been amicable, became frosty. In order to attempt to repair the strained relationship, Temujin went so far as to offer to marry Jochi to one of Toghrul's daughters, but Toghrul refused. It was a gross and calculated insult, though also possibly a consequence of the doubts men harbored about Jochi's parentage, and it drove Temujin into a fury. Instead of an amicable settlement of the dispute, there would be war.

Toghrul was wary of Temujin's new Mongol federation and of Temujin's ability as a commander, so he sought to even the odds by allying himself with Jamukha. Though Jamukha maintained respect and affection for his blood-brother, the two had been rivals for quite some time, even if this was to be the first major clash between the two. However, Jamukha proved to be as intractable an ally for Toghrul as he had been for Temujin, and the two rapidly fell out, their situation worsened by the fact a number of important tribes notionally loyal to their newly formed coalition deserted to Temujin. Toghrul and Jamukha were defeated, and though Jamukha and a sizeable number of his followers managed to flee, the Kerait as an independent federation was finished. They were incorporated into the new Mongol federation, and their surviving warriors went on to swell the ranks of Temujin's ever-burgeoning army.

Temujin now turned his attention to Jamukha, who had fled west into the lands of the Naiman federation along with what was left of his army and followers. The Naimans, led by Kuchlug, along with what remained of the Merkits, convened a *kurultai* (council of Khans) and elected Jamukha their Gur Khan (Great Leader). Temujin, with his well-publicized aspirations of Mongolian unification, could not ignore such a deliberate slap in the face, and in 1201 he marched on Jamukha and his new allies. Before battle was even joined, his ranks were swollen by thousands of deserters who reckoned they would benefit from serving in Temujin's new, meritocratic army. Among these deserters was Subotai, a general and a notorious soldier who was also the younger brother of Jelme, one of Temujin's generals and earliest supporters.

In another unusual custom, Temujin's army accepted deserters and treated them better than defeated warriors and captured enemies. While deserters were welcomed, defeated warriors and captured enemies were, for apparently the first time, treated ruthlessly; they were "measured against the linchpin", which meant they were forced to march past a wagon wheel. If they were taller than the wagon wheel (meaning they were fully grown and not yet stooped by age), they were beheaded, ostensibly to prevent tribal rivalries that might be nourished by not-easily-indoctrinated adults.

Temujin clashed with Jamukha in half a dozen battles, and though none of them were decisive Jamukha nonetheless racked up a string of defeats over the years that led his frustrated followers to hand him over to Temujin in 1206. This move backfired, as Temujin, declaring that he would not abide disloyal men in his army, had Jamukha's betrayers publicly executed. He also offered to renew his friendship with Jamukha, promising a place of high regard in his army, but Jamukha, humbled by his defeat, instead begged for an honorable execution. According to Mongolian tradition, an honorable execution had to be a bloodless one, and Temujin granted his wish.

The war was not yet over with Jamukha's defeat, but it was almost done. What was left of the Merkits were defeated piecemeal by Subotai, newly promoted to the rank of general in Temujin's army and quickly justifying the trust reposed in him and the reputation as an able commander he had acquired among the ranks of Temujin's enemies. The Khan of the Naiman federation, Kuchlug, realized that all hope was lost and fled west to the lands of the Kara-Khitai Khanate, which still remained independent and hostile to Temujin. However, they must have felt quite lonely, for they were virtually alone in retaining their independence. In the space of just a few years, by hook or by crook, Temujin had united the Naimans, the Merkits, the Tatars, the Uyghurs, and the Keraits into a single Mongol federation, a feat unheard of in living memory. At a *kurultai* sometime after 1206, Temujin was proclaimed by the assembled Khans to be Genghis Khan, Great Khan of all the Mongols.

A medieval depiction of Genghis Khan being proclaimed Khagan of all Mongols

Having already accomplished something none of his contemporaries had thought possible, Genghis could have been content with what he had achieved, but he was far from done. He had promised his people more, including the plunder of China, and he would make good on that promise.

Though there seems to have been some earlier contacts with Chinese dynasties through Toghrul Khan, and the Chinese were certainly aware of and probably worried by Temujin's activities, his involvement in the affairs of the ever-feuding Chinese dynasties began directly in 1205 when a group of renegade Mongols from the Kerait tribe took refuge with the Xi Xia Dynasty in what is now north-western China. Because the Xi Xia had agreed to give the Keraits aid, Genghis launched an attack on their territory, forcing several of the local noblemen to acknowledge him as overlord. However, at the time Genghis was still preoccupied with defeating Jamukha and uniting Mongolia, so this initial incursion into Chinese territory was aborted.

Once he had united the Mongols, however, Genghis returned to the domains of the Xi Xia in 1207, and this time he came with a vengeance. He quickly sacked the fortress of Wulahai, one of the main Xi Xia garrisons, after capturing it by subterfuge and annexing the surrounding region. There was a lull in the fighting between 1207-1209, but hostilities were violently renewed when Genghis launched an invasion with a host of around 70,000 Mongol infantry and cavalry, the core of which were his feared horse archers, warriors that conventional forces had significant trouble dealing with. Their double-curved bows were immensely powerful despite their compact size, almost as much as English longbows, and they could shoot them as easily from the saddle as they could from foot. Just as importantly, the horse archers were so skilled on horses that they could ride in at a gallop to shower slow-moving formations with a hail of arrows before veering quickly out of the way of a counterattack. They were devastating in the open field and could be counted upon to destroy any enemy no matter how heavily armored, for heavy armor just made them slower to maneuver. However, the Mongol cavalry was useless in attacking fortifications, and the Xi Xia were quick to seize upon this fact and try to use it to their full advantage.

In 1211, Genghis Khan summoned a *kurultai* to confirm the declaration of war, and that same year he launched his great army, numbering around 100,000 warriors, against the Jin, who were rumored to have as many as a million men under arms themselves. Genghis Khan's army was entirely cavalry, either armored heavy cavalry or horse archers, and it traveled with no commissariat or supply train, meaning it was immensely mobile.

The Mongols first fought a series of indecisive clashes with the vastly superior (around 400,000 men) Chinese forces which, though not important to the war's outcome, nonetheless allowed generals like Jebe The Arrow, Muqali and Subotai ample opportunity to distinguish themselves alongside Tolui and Ogadai, two of Genghis's sons who had been entrusted with armies of their own.

Eventually, the Mongol army advanced towards the narrow defile of Badger Pass in the Zhangjiakou region. The Mongols, in typical fashion, had scourged and harrowed all the lands west of Badger Pass, which was the last natural defensive position of any strength west of the vast city of Zhongdu (modern Beijing, and the seat of the Jin Emperor). Heisilie Hushashu, the general in charge of the Jin forces, which thanks to an emergency call-up from every town and garrison in the Jin domains now numbered 500,000 men, knew his business: Badger Pass would negate the advantage of Mongol maneuverability by forcing the horse archers to loose their volleys and ride their horses within tight confines. This would force the fight into a hand-to-hand struggle, which would favor Jin's tactics and weaponry.

Depiction of fighting at Badger Pass

However, by this time the Mongols had started equipping themselves with Chinese steel cuirasses and even manufacturing their own, and their cavalry was heavily armored and protected enough to engage in hand-to-hand fighting. Moreover, prior to the battle's commencement, Genghis, displaying magnificent tactical acumen, dispatched lightly armored men to scale the heights around Badger Pass and encircle the enemy army, attacking them from the rear at the same time Genghis advanced the main bulk of his army up the Pass. Despite the lack of space to manuever, the Mongol warriors proved their superiority to the Jin conscripts and professionals and the encircled Jin army was utterly destroyed, the scattered survivors harried by the rampaging Mongol cavalry for more than 30 miles. The Jin general fled to Zhongdu, where he murdered the Jin Emperor and assumed control of the city, naming his nephew Wanyang Xun Emperor.

Meanwhile, Genghis detached a force under Jebe to invade and harry Manchuria, where they captured the city of Shenyang. By 1212, even though Genghis had suffered a wound in the interim, the Mongols were masters of Manchuria and were ready to lay siege to Zhongdu itself in the very center of the Jin heartland. Despite some of his detachments suffering a defeat against a scratch mobile column of Jin forces, Genghis and his generals smashed the Jin armies in the field to shreds and ravaged the now undefended Chinese plains before besieging Zhongdu in 1214.

Once again, Genghis found it difficult to invest a Chinese stronghold. Throughout a protracted siege, Genghis was unable to reduce the city walls, but the situation inside of them got so desperate that the defenders were eventually forced to the point of starvation and began eating their own dead. On top of that, their general, Heishilie Husashu, lost his life. Eventually the Jin surrendered Zhongdu and agreed to pay Genghis a colossal tribute, the likes of which had never been seen, and the Jin also presented him with a princess in marriage. Satisfied, enriched, and having proven who was the better ruler, Genghis withdrew his army.

Persuaded that Zhongdu was not the impregnable stronghold he had envisaged, Wanyang Xun moved the Jin capital further from the ravages of the Mongols to the southern city of Kaifeng. However, in 1215 one of the Jin armies defected to Genghis's side, and apparently without instigation they launched an attack on Zhongdu. Taking advantage of the situation, Genghis sent a fresh Mongol army against Zhongdu, and the city was ruthlessly sacked in May of that year. The loss of Zhongdu and the surrender of one of the larger Jin field armies in the area broke the back of the Jin resistance, and in the following years (1215-1217) the Mongol armies mopped up what was left of their resistance in most of the northern Jin territories, adding them to the burgeoning Mongol Empire.

Depiction of Mongol cavalry fighting Jin warriors

Though the mopping up would take years, Genghis was now effectively in control of most of the region, and in addition to territorial gains and a vast amount of wealth, Genghis and his army also gained a massive wealth of invaluable experience and expertise. The subjugation of western China brought better armor and better blacksmithing techniques for Mongol warriors, a host of logicians and supply experts who could provide Genghis's army with lines of communication and supply stretching for thousands of miles, and hundreds if not thousands of vastly skilled Chinese military engineers who knew how to manufacture and operate siege weapons the like of which the Mongols had never seen before. No fortress, no matter how large or sophisticated, would ever again be a match for them.

In late 1227, following the destruction of the Tangut dynasty, Genghis Khan himself died. His death is shrouded in mystery and hounded by controversy, but several popular theories exist. One ancient account claimed a Tangut princess whom Genghis had either been given in marriage or was intent on assaulting pulled out a knife she had concealed and stabbed him in the groin or leg, leading to his death from blood loss or gangrene. The princess was then said to have thrown herself into the Yellow River afterwards to preserve her virtue. This extremely demeaning death is most likely a fiction, the result of negative propaganda from hostile chroniclers after Genghis's death.

Other more likely accounts suggest that Genghis was killed in a final battle against the Tanguts or suffered a fall from a horse, either during a military action or during a hunt, and that it aggravated his old wounds and eventually killed him. Some believe he suffered from some debilitating disease, such as pneumonia or tuberculosis, which eventually finished the elderly Khan off. It is worth noting that at this point Genghis was in his mid-to-late 60s and had been fighting virtually uninterruptedly for the better part of 50 years, so it is highly likely that decades of campaigning would have taken their toll, making even a trivial injury or illness potentially life-threatening.

After Genghis Khan's death, his body was brought east to the Mongolian heartland, where pursuant to his wishes he was buried near his birthplace in a secret, unmarked location, per Mongolian custom. His funeral guard killed anyone they met on the way to his burial site, so no one would know where Genghis's bones lay, and then stampeded their horses repeatedly over the spot to give no indication of where he was buried. Some versions of this story even suggest a river was diverted over the site.

Following his death, Genghis's sons enacted the provisions laid out by his will, which he had planned meticulously in the years following the campaign against the Khwarezmid Empire. The Mongol army, numbering over 130,000 men, was split up among his family, with the bulk (around 100,000 men) going to Tolui as the youngest, while the remaining 30,000 men went to his other male children (who all had sizeable forces of their own already). Genghis's empire was also split up, though it remained a Mongol empire with intimately connected family and cultural ties, in accordance to his wishes. Ogadai, his favorite son, received the title of Great Khan and the Empire of the Great Khan, comprising most of Eastern Asia and China; Tolui, the youngest, received the Mongolian Heartland; Genghis's grandsons Batu and Orda, Jochi's sons, received the western Eurasian territories, including eastern Rus; and Chagatai was given Central Asia and Khwarezm. All of them would build upon Genghis's legacy, using the Yassa code of governance and the administrative and military infrastructure he had created to expand his territories further than they had ever stretched. In 1279, about 50 years after Genghis's death, the empire he had started and built from scratch stretched from Poland to Korea.

The Origins of the Golden Horde

Under Ogedei, the already massive empire, which spanned the Mongolian heartlands and central Asia to the Caspian Sea, extended even further into Khwarazmian Persia and the Russian steppes. By the 1240s, Mongol horsemen had crossed the Danube and the Grand Principality of Novgorod had submitted to the Mongols as their vassal. On August 9, 1241, a Mongol horde of several thousand horse archers met a similar number of Polish and Moravian knights at Liegnitz (Modern Legnica, southwestern Poland). The result was a decisive Mongol victory.

The Hungarians had been defeated at the Battle of Mohi four months earlier, and the Mongols were now poised to invade Germany and Italy, but in the end, they didn't. In December 1241, the Great Khan died, and the first princes of the empire journeyed to the imperial capital, Karakorum, to elect his successor. One of these was Batu, a grandson of Genghis Khan through his first son Jochi. Genghis had assigned him the appanage of central Asia and the Russian steppes which he governed with the title Khan, subordinate to the Great Khan in Karakorum. His regime came to be called the Golden Horde, and in Mongolian, *Altan Ord.* The English word "horde" invokes a colorful image of savage warriors though the Mongolian word means a palace or camp. "Golden" may refer to the gold color of the Mongols' tents or to an actual tent used by Batu.[2] It is also possible that "Golden" is a transliteration of the Mongolian word for yellow, which may also mean "center," in which case Golden Horde meant "Central Camp."[3] The domain of Batu has also been known as the Kipchak Khanate (after the Turkic peoples, also known as Cumans, who inhabited central Asia) and the Ulus (Realm) of Jochi.

---

[2] Atwood, Christopher Pratt (2004). *Empire, Facts* on File p.201.
[3] Gleason, Abbott (2009). *A Companion to Russian History*. John Wiley & Sons. p. 82.

A medieval Chinese depiction of Batu Khan

The Golden Horde was divided into two further hordes. The Blue Horde spanned the Russian steppes and encompassed the lands of the Turkic Cumans (Kipchaks) and the Bulgars who settled in the Volga region and the realm of the Iranian Alans in the Caucasus. These lands were directly ruled by Batu. East of the Volga lay the vast plains of central Asia, ruled by Batu's brother Orda.

As senior khan, Batu established his court at Sarai on the Akhtuba River, a tributary of the Volga and about 130 kilometers northwest of the Volga Delta flowing into the Caspian Sea. It was principally Batu and Orda who led armies into Russia and the rest of Eastern Europe. In fact, Batu was invading Austria when the news of Ogedei's death reached him.

The princes arrived in Karakorum to discover that the government was in the hands of

Ogedei's widow, Khatun Toregene, who was scheming to prepare the throne for her son Guyuk. However, the late Great Khan had wanted his grandson Siremum (his son by another wife) to succeed, and although the great princes confirmed her in the regency, they did not agree upon the succession. Toregene appealed to Batu for help, but he remained at Sarai, pleading his inability to leave on account of gout. The fact was that he did not want Toregene's son to be placed upon the throne, in part because he and Guyuk had quarreled over strategy in Eastern Europe. The latter had publicly insulted Batu, for which he would have been degraded and humiliated in an equally public manner by his father had not the Great Khan died before he could do so. Even so, Guyuk blamed Batu for his loss of status within the imperial clan. It was therefore in Batu's interests to delay the election as long as he could, while in the meantime strengthening the Golden Horde under his leadership. Toregene, a masterful politician and administrator in her own right, also decided to use the delay to consolidate power for her son and to persuade the other Mongol princes to elect him.

When the *kurultai* could be delayed no longer, Batu did not come personally but sent envoys, perhaps fearing that an elected Guyuk would remove him from his position. If so, he need not have feared greatly, because even though Guyuk was elected by the majority of the princes in 1246, he was not powerful enough to move against his enemies. His mother was reluctant to relinquish power, and when she died, he felt compelled to dismiss her unpopular ministers and replace them with the trusted servants of his father.

Guyuk was an able enough ruler but insecure, and he was especially wary of Batu, who had been exercising authority over the Russian princes on his own authority. Guyuk must have felt threatened when he learned that Batu had confirmed Grand Prince Yaroslav II of Vladimir as suzerain of all the other Russian princes, and when Batu confirmed David VI as King of Georgia, Guyuk pointedly gave the crown to David's rival. Moreover, he began reversing many of Batu's government appointments.

A medieval portrait of Guyuk

Guyuk decided to bring the clash with Batu to a head, so he summoned the Khan of the Golden Horde. Batu obeyed and made toward Karakorum, but with a substantial army. No doubt fearing that Batu meant to depose him, Guyuk marched westward to meet him, but he died on the journey on April 20, 1248 at the age of 42.

Batu was now, at the age of 43, the senior Mongol prince and had ruled the Golden Horde for 21 years. He used his seniority to convene the *kurultai* within his own territory and it duly offered the crown to him. He unexpectedly declined the honor however. Possibly he was content with the Golden Horde and simply wished to ensure that the descendants of Ogedei, whom he distrusted, did not rule.[4] More probably he realized that he would not be able to hold the entire empire given the divisions between his own branch of the imperial family, the Jochians, the Toluids, descendants of Genghis's son Tolui, represented at the *kurultai* by Prince Mongke, and

---
[4] George Lane, Genghis Khan and Mongol Rule, xxxvii.

the Ogedeians.

Batu's choice of Great Khan was Mongke, and he was elected by another *kurultai*, this time at Kodoe Aral in Mongolia but still under Batu's patronage. Batu's decision may have been calculated to provoke a civil war, which would have consolidated his own power over the Golden Horde. If so, it succeeded, as the Ogedeians and other branches of the imperial house rose against Mongke and were defeated. The Golden Horde supported Mongke, and Batu was subsequently confirmed as viceroy over the western empire.

Mongke continued the conquest of northern and western China and further expanded into Mesopotamia, Asia Minor, Tibet, and Korea. By the time the Great Khan died in 1259, Batu had been dead four years. He was succeeded briefly, as Khan of the Golden Horde by his son Sartak (d. 1257), only to be replaced in turn by a brother (or son), Ulagchi, who survived less than a year. Berke, a brother of Batu, followed, and he distinguished himself from other princes of the Golden Horde in being a Muslim. The ancestral worship of the Mongols was Shamanist in character and generally tolerant of other religions. Islam, on the other hand, was not so reconciliatory and had been spread mainly at the point of a sword.

Berke's first encounter with the faith of Mohammed occurred in Sarai when he conversed with Muslim traders from the central Asian city of Bukhara. When he became khan, he set about creating an Islamic state, forcing the majority of the Blue Horde (over whom the descendants of Batu had direct oversight) to convert to his new religion. Berke's zeal brought him into conflict with the new Great Khan, the renowned Kublai (r.1260-1294) when he went to war with Kublai's ally, Halagu, Khan of Persia, over the sack of Baghdad in 1258. Baghdad was considered one of the great cities of Islam, and Halagu's barbarity outraged the Khan of the Golden Horde.

The war between the two Mongol princes, which took place mainly in the Caucasus, came almost immediately after a war for the throne between Kublai and his allies and the Toluids. These conflicts highlighted serious divisions within the empire - the Golden Horde refused to recognize Kublai, and none of the khans attended a *kurultai* to confirm the accession. Kublai held immediate sway over only Mongolia, China, and the east, and he seemed to realize that the Mongolian Empire had irremediably fractured when he moved the imperial capital from Karakorum to Khanbalik (modern Beijing) in 1264, adopted Buddhism as the state religion, and identified himself with the emperors of China. When he died at the age of 78 on February 18, 1294, none of the three western khans journeyed to Khanbalik to elect a successor.

A portrait of Kublai Khan

At this point, the Mongol Empire was essentially divided into four independent realms consisting of China, the Golden Horde, Ilkhanate (Persia) and Chagatai (Central Asia).

The Golden Horde's Government and Society

Berke did not live to see the formal end of the Mongol Empire. This distinction, if it was considered one at the time, went to Toqta (r. 1291–1312), a great grandson of Batu. He was a Tengrist, as Islam had not yet gained dominion over the princes of the Golden Horde, but this changed in 1312 when Toqta's nephew Uzbeg ascended the throne. Like Berke, he had been converted to Islam after contact with Bukharan Muslims and, like his predecessor, meant to impose Islam as the state religion. In this he was opposed by a coalition of Tengrist and Buddhist nobles, whom he crushed mercilessly. He thereupon commanded all the Mongol nobility to convert to Islam, and he resolved to turn his realm into a monarchy based on the principles of Islamic law.

Uzbeg adopted the new name Mohammed and styled himself "The Succorer of the Faith."[5] He did not attempt to forcibly covert his Christian and Buddhist subjects, but he implemented the common practice of protecting non-Muslims as long as they paid the *jizyah*, a tax enjoined by the Koran, higher than that imposed upon Muslims. Although he continued to be addressed as Khan, he took two Muslim titles: *Sultan* and *Shahanshah*. The latter is translated "King of Kings" and was borrowed from the rulers of Persia. Sultan comes from Arabic and carries with it religious significance, denoting a ruler who is the recipient of both secular and religious authority. It was used by Muslim monarchs who claimed supreme authority without assuming the office of Caliph, the temporal and spiritual leader of all Muslims.

In Uzbeg, the Mongol and Muslim concepts of monarchy were fused. In the Mongol model the Great Khan or *Khagan,* a descendant of Genghis, was empowered to carry out the divine mandate, i.e. to bring the entire world under the dominion of the Enduring Sky (the sky spirit, Tengri). All the members of the imperial house (*Altan Urugh*) shared in this mandate,[6] and the senior clan leaders met in the *kurultai* to elect the Great Khan and to organize the campaigns needed to carry them out. In the Islamic model the ruler was the guardian of the Islamic order as mandated by God through Mohammed and the Koran. His power was not therefore absolute but limited by Islamic law. He was advised and guided by the religious consensus of lay jurists and might even be deposed if he failed in his duty to protect the *Ummah*, the Islamic community. One of his principle duties was military, undertaking *jihad* to defend Islam and even to extend it into the lands of unbelievers.[7] The Islamic additions to the Mongolian monarchy thus produced an institution of potentially awesome power.

The term "Golden Horde" itself did not appear until the 16th century,[8] and the Mongols themselves referred to their territories as the *Ulus* (realm) of Jochi, one of the sons of Genghis Khan. Others generally referred to it as the Kipchak Khanate, referring to the Turkic tribespeople who inhabited the steppes when the Mongols arrived. As stated before, the Golden Horde was divided into two regions. The White Horde, ruled by the direct descendants of Batu Khan (who was always the Sultan), extended from the Volga west to the Prut and the borders of Moldavia. It extended into Caucasia and north to the lands of the Bulgars who inhabited the confluence between the Volga and Kama rivers. The Blue Horde spanned Central Asia from the Caspian Sea to Lake Baikal. This was ruled by the descendants of Batu's brother Orda who bore the title Khan but in a capacity subordinate to the ruler of the Blue Horde.

The *kurultai* remained after Islam was introduced as the highest consultative body and the institution that elected the sultan's successor from the descendants of Genghis Khan. The chief minister of state was the *beklare-bek*, and he assumed both the civil and military administration.

---

[5] Henry Hoyle Howorth (1876), *History of the Mongols from the 9th to the 19th century; The So-called Tartars of Russia and Central Asia*, Cosimo Inc., p.172.
[6] Including women. The widows of khans were habitually regents until the kurultai elected a successor.
[7] Peters, Rudolph; Cook, David (2014). "Jihād". *The Oxford Encyclopedia of Islam and Politics*. Oxford: Oxford University Press.
[8] Lawrence N. Langer (2001), *Historical Dictionary of Medieval Russia*, Scarecrow Press p.53.

Indeed, in Mongol society there was no division between the roles. Following the tradition in Islamic states, viziers were appointed to assist the monarch in the administration of the Realm (*Ulug*). The imperial court sent *basqaqs* into the provinces to collect taxes, maintain order, and deal with local issues. They were not governors in the direct sense, though they are often named so, the Mongols being content to permit local institutions of government to persist, as long as they kept the population subservient.

The Mongol chieftains, all descendants of Batu or Orda, constituted the aristocracy of the Golden Horde, whereas the general population consisted mostly of Mongols and Turkic peoples (Cumans,[9] Kipchaks, Bulgars and Khwarezmians). These were often collectively named *Tatars* by Russians and other Eastern Europeans, who frequently added an extra letter to make it *tartar*, meaning an inhabitant of *Tartarus* or Hell.

Beyond the immediate government of the Horde were the vassals, states that were permitted to preserve their autonomy in return for regular tribute. The princes of these states were granted charters or *yarliks* to rule in the name of the khan, and each new ruler had to seek confirmation from him. Failure to carry out the khan's wishes or render tribute could result in the harshest punishment.

The vast lands of Russia, divided into many principalities, were all subject to the Golden Horde, as well as Wallachia, Circassia and Albania in the Caucasus, and the Venetian ports of the Crimea.

---

[9] Hence the name "Cumania" which is sometimes applied to the steppes where the Golden Horde ruled.

A map of the Golden Horde

Meanwhile, the city of Sarai was the chief city of the Golden Horde and one of the greatest cities of medieval times. It had around 70 000 inhabitants at a time when a city of 10 000 was considered large. In fact, there were two cities named Sarai that successively served as capitals: the first was established by Batu Khan; the second by Berke nearby (the exact location of either is uncertain). Sarai was an important trading center as it lay on the caravan route from the Black Sea to central Asia. Through Persia it also provided access to the goods of the Middle East and through the sea lanes to Egypt, Venice and Genoa. It was also an important culture center, the Mongols being generally tolerant of all religions as long as their adherents paid their taxes and offered tribute regularly.

The city was not strictly Mongolian, being divided into districts – Mongol, Alan, Cuman and Russian – each with their own administrations, markets and centers of worship. It might be imagined as a truly multi-ethnic city, as many Islamic and Mongolian cities were, where a visitor might expect to see individuals from every place in the known world.

Strangely enough, however, the one person a visitor might not spy on was the Khan himself, for he tended to follow the custom of his ancestors, living a nomadic existence in the imperial *ordo* (palace), a complex of tents likened to a mobile city, in the vicinity of Sarai in winter and in the steppes in summer. Indeed, none of the Mongol chieftains and their tribes settled permanently in their *Ulug* – not as would be understood in European culture – preferring the nomadic and pastoral lifestyle observed by their ancestors for hundreds of years (and still by many Mongols today). The khan drew his ministers and governors from the ranks of the *keshik*, the elite imperial bodyguard numbering about 10,000. This practice ensured in theory the integrity of government, as every appointee would be known and vetted by the imperial court. These were attached to the imperial *ordo* and did not permanently reside in the territories they administered. Thus, Sarai was not a capital city in the sense that might be understood in the West; that is, it was not strictly a seat of government.

It has been mentioned that there was no distinction made in Mongol society between the civilian and military classes, and in fact, there is no word for "soldier" in the medieval Mongol language.[10] That said, Genghis Khan and his successors adapted the skills of the nomadic horsemen, (riding, hunting, herding, foraging and migrating) to the challenges of building an empire. The Great Khan organized them decimally, with an *arban* of 10 being the smallest unit and the *tumen* of 10,000 being the largest. No warrior was permitted to transfer from one unit to another, ensuring that armies separated by hundreds of miles could operate autonomously. Moreover, these armies were never dispersed; even in times of peace; they migrated through the land, following pasture. They did not require money from the imperial treasury to be maintained,

---

[10]Dattatraya Mandal 2019)("Mongols, the armies, organization, armor and tactics", *Realm of History* https://www.realmofhistory.com/2019/01/25/mongols-nomads-largest-land-empire/.

for each clan was responsible for keeping itself in a battle-ready condition. Thus, whenever there was a rebellion or an invasion, it was already prepared for combat.

History has greatly exaggerated the size of the Golden Horde. The English word "horde" conjures up an image of numberless warriors charging recklessly into battle, but the Golden Horde numbered no larger than 35,000 when it invaded Russia in 1237[11] and always represented a small proportion of the population of the *Ulug* and its vassals. Nevertheless, they employed auxiliaries, usually from the Turkic peoples who were nomadic horsemen like themselves, and these swelled their numbers in large campaigns. They were also skilled in making their numbers appear much larger than they were, employing such methods as setting dummy warriors on horses and increasing clouds of dust by tying sticks to the tails of their mounts.

The Golden Horde, as with every Mongol army, was skilled in scouting and gathering intelligence before encountering a foe. They also infamously used terror to cow their enemies and maintain order. Enemy troops and inhabitants of the towns and countryside, whether military or civilian, were habitually slaughtered and their dwellings razed to the ground, though they did not usually torture their victims. This savagery was never uncontrolled however, and the Mongols were actually noted for their discipline. Film and television depictions of Mongol cavalry uttering brutish cries as they swarm shapelessly toward the enemy are incorrect - they marched in columns and arrayed themselves in battle positions to the sound of enormous war drums borne by camels. Commands were communicated by means of banners, and it was only when the order to charge had been given that they screamed to intimidate the enemy.

Mongol cavalrymen were of two grades: light and heavy. Both were skilled in the use of the composite bow, with the more heavily armored also using maces, sabers, and lances. Mongol horses were small but sturdy and hardy, so they were better able to survive extremes of climate and to forage on little food. They were not as fast as their Western counterparts, however, further dispelling the myth of fast movement.

The heavy cavalry were shock troops, with both rider and mount suited in lamellar, overlapping plates of iron or bronze bound by leather. They bore lances with hooked blades when charging in order to gouge or unseat enemy cavalry. Swifter horseman would then follow, hacking at survivors. An attack was preceded by a rain of armor-piercing arrows fired by bows with a range of 250 meters, twice that of English longbows. Mongol horse archers could fire six arrows a minute. Arrows were of varying designs, some for inflicting severe wounds, others for killing cleanly or even making whistling sounds in the air to terrify the enemy. Some arrowheads were dipped in naphtha and set alight.

A favorite battle tactic was the feigned retreat, employed by many armies in many situations. A unit of cavalry would pretend to flee, only to draw the pursuing force into a deadly trap.

---

[11]Leo de Hartog (2004), *Genghis Khan: Conqueror of the World*, Tauris Parke pp. 165–66.

The Mongols could not conquer nations without taking their cities, and unlike many of the Turkic tribesmen of their time, they mastered the art of siege warfare. They absorbed the technology from the Chinese, Persians, and Arabs, constructing catapults, mangonels, trebuchets, ballistae, and siege towers. Some scholars even credit the Golden Horde with using gunpowder weapons during the invasion of Russia, which took place a century before guns were used by Western militaries.[12]

In other words, the success of the Golden Horde was due to its meticulous organization and tribal unity, its mastery of military tactics (particularly horsemanship and archery), and its use of terror. These skills allowed the Golden Horde to secure dominion over a population many times its size. Moreover, it must be remembered that the Horde accomplished this without a permanent administrative infrastructure - the entire horde, including the imperial court, moved constantly, and yet it was able to maintain control of its vast holdings and vassals for over 200 years.

The Horde Under Uzbeg

Sultan-Khan Uzbeg (r.1313–1341) was the longest-reigning and probably the most able of the monarchs of the Golden Horde, and his success was due in no small part to his adoption of Islam as the state religion. Islam emphasized the unity of society in one discipline of faith and behaviour and under one ruler, considered "The Shadow of God upon Earth."[13] As mentioned earlier, Uzbeg enjoined Islam upon all the Mongol princes and their clans, and while he did not force Islam upon the subject peoples of the Horde, he did invite missionaries to come and instruct them in the ways of the Prophet, and resistance was met with violence. When Ilbasan, Khan of the White Horde, refused to abandon the religion of his forbears, Uzbeg replaced him with his Muslim brother, Mubarack Khwaja, in 1320.

Uzbeg's accession coincided with a power struggle between the Chagatai Khanate and the Chinese Khanate, with the Persian-based Ilkhanate supporting China. Khan Esen Buqa I of the Chagatai attempted to draw Uzbeg into the conflict by suggesting that the Emperor of China, who still claimed a pre-eminent position over the other four khanates, meant to depose him. The Khan of the Golden Horde, engaged in putting down anti-Islamic rebellions, would not intervene.

Sound as this policy may have been, Uzbeg decided that the Ilkhanate needed to be dealt with because its victory over the Chagatai made it a rival to the Golden Horde. Having consolidated his power domestically, he invaded Azerbaijan in 1319. The Mongols of Persia, like the Jochids of the Golden Horde, had converted to Islam, but the other great Muslim power of the Middle East, the Mamluk Sultanate of Egypt, preferred to ally itself with Uzbeg. Though initially successful, the invasion failed, due largely to a reconciliation between Cairo and Khan Abu Said

---

[12] Mende, Tibor (1944). *Hungary*. Macdonald & Co. Ltd. p. 34.
[13] "Shadow of God." In *The Oxford Dictionary of Islam*. Ed. John L. Esposito. *Oxford Islamic Studies Online*. 01-Dec-2019.

in 1323. Thereafter, Uzbeg was forced to withdraw and negotiate a peace.

The Ilkhanate's victories in the Caucasus belied its power, however. When Abu Said died in 1335, the empire descended into civil war and splintered into a number of independent states. The threat to the southern borders of the Golden Horde was thus removed.

During the wars with the Ilkhanate, Uzbeg did not turn his attention away from the West. One of his objectives was to weaken the Balkans and prevent one single power dominating the region, and to this end the Golden Horde raided the rich lands of the Byzantine Empire, principally Thrace, in 1319, in support of the rulers of Bulgaria and Serbia. The domains of Byzantine Emperor Andronicus III were also under attack by a new and rising Muslim state, the Ottoman Empire, and the emperor was naturally anxious to secure a peace. He offered his illegitimate daughter to Uzbeg, who called her Bayalun. The marriage added to the prestige of the sultan, but when she returned to her father in 1324, fearful that she might be forced to convert, the Horde pillaged Thrace for 55 days and took 300,000 captives.

The Kingdom of Hungary, growing stronger under the centralizing influence of the Angevins, was also a potential threat. In 1326 the Golden Horde launched a savage raid against Hungary in support of the Voivode of Wallachia, Basarab I (r.1310-1352), who had revolted against his overlord, King Charles I of Hungary (r.1308 – 1342). Basarab destroyed the Hungarian army at the Battle of Posada (1330) and secured Wallachia's independence. This was of great advantage to the Golden Horde, for Hungary was denied access to the Black Sea and thus the opportunity of disrupting the trade route to Sarai.

At the same time the Horde was securing its Balkan borders, the seeds of strife were being sown in Russia. As noted earlier, the vast lands of the Rus, from the Carpathian Mountains in the south to Novgorod in the north, had been conquered by the Golden Horde. When the Horde first invaded in 1237, the Grand Prince of Kiev was nominally ruler of this vast empire, but the Slavic empire had been severely weakened by internal divisions. The invasion shattered what little internal cohesion remained. The Kievan army was annihilated and the cities of Russia razed to the ground and its inhabitants massacred. Only the cities of Novgorod and Pskov were spared, and only because they surrendered. By 1242 the entire land lay burning and in ruins, and it is estimated that some 500,000 perished, which may have been about 7% of the population of Russia.[14]

All the while, the Mongols were not interested in colonizing the lands of the Rus. Instead, they appointed local rulers who collected taxes and tribute on behalf of the khan and ensured that his wishes were observed. Thus, the Russian principalities continued to be governed by their own laws, and their religion – Eastern Orthodox Christianity – was preserved and even protected. These principalities were often rivals for the favor of their overlords, and their rulers might be

---

[14] Colin McEvedy, *Atlas of World Population History* (1978) http://necrometrics.com/pre1700a.htm.

denounced to the Golden Horde by princes anxious to supplant them, which suited the Golden Horde very well. After all, if the Russian princes fought each other, they would not be united against the invaders.

The Princes of Tver, a city on the Volga River, were in a contest with the Princes of Moscow for the leadership of the Grand Principality of Vladimir-Suzdal, located in northwest Russia and providing a link between the wealthy trading city of Novgorod and Sarai. The ruler of Vladimir-Suzdal was recognized as the premier prince of the Rus, and Tver and Moscow vied for the title which was in the gift of the khan. The Grand Prince was nominally lord of all Russia as the khan's representative and responsible for the collection of taxes and tribute, a duty that gave him considerable power and wealth.

In 1325 Prince Yuri of Moscow was Grand Prince. He was on good terms with Khan Uzbeg and married to his sister Konchaka, and he used his position to make war upon his rival Mikhail of Tver. After he failed to defeat him militarily, he falsely accused him of the death of Konchaka, whereupon Uzbeg summoned both leaders to Sarai. After a trial, Mikhail was executed by being trampled to death by horses.

Mikhail had been popular amongst the Rus and Yuri found it difficult to collect revenue for the khan. Moreover, Mikhail's son Dimitry, called "The Terrible Eyed," accused Yuri of keeping a large portion of the revenue due to the Golden Horde for himself. Whether Yuri was guilty is impossible to say, but Uzbeg was sufficiently persuaded to summon him to Sarai. The Prince of Moscow encountered his accuser in the city, and both were called to give an account of themselves before Uzbeg. The sultan seemed deaf to Yuri's protestations of innocence and made Dimitry Grand Prince of Russia without bothering to withdraw Yuri's own charter. There were in effect then two Grand Princes. Perhaps Uzbeg did not readily accept Dimitry's tale of deceit and corruption, and it is probable that he deliberately set one prince against the other in order to weaken Russia

Indeed, this notion would seem to be supported by the events that followed. In 1324, Grand Prince Yuri set out for Sarai again with the intention of laying denunciations of Dimitry before the sultan. Grand Prince Dimitry followed him there and accused him of his father's murder and slew him on the spot.

Uzbeg, who could not allow the murder of a Grand Prince, had Dimitry detained for a year before he was executed in the same manner as his father had been. Uzbeg's scheme to divide and weaken the Rus had failed dismally, and now he had to appoint a new Grand Prince. When Dimitry's younger brother Alexander appeared in Sarai to claim both the Principality of Tver and the Grand Principality of Vladimir-Suzdal, Uzbeg granted his wish, leaving Ivan I of Moscow, Yuri's brother, furious.

Uzbeg's appointment may have been calculated to weaken the power of the Grand Princes, for

Alexander proved an ineffectual monarch. He seemed incapable of ruling the other Russian princes and more seriously, of collecting revenue for the Golden Horde. In 1327 Uzbeg's cousin, Shevkal, was sent as an emissary to demand the Sultan's due, and probably in a deliberate attempt to provoke the Rus, took up residence in Alexander's palace and began terrorizing Tver. The populace responded in kind, massacring the Tatar envoys and burning Shevkal and his soldiers alive.

This uprising was the first serious attempt of the Russian people to throw off the yoke of the Golden Horde, and Alexander had no intention of leading it. Knowing what the Mongols would do to himself and the city, he fled to the Republic of Pskov, then an independent state bordering the Grand Duchy of Lithuania and the Baltic territories under the rule of the Teutonic Knights. Not only did the inhabitants of that city accept him, but they made him their prince.

In the meantime, Uzbeg, no doubt believing it worse to employ Russians to punish Russians, made Ivan of Moscow Grand Prince and commissioned him to inflict the imperial vengeance on Tver and its allies, as well as to pursue Alexander. At the instigation of Grand Prince Ivan, the Metropolitan of All Rus, Theognostus, excommunicated the Republic of Pskov ahead of an invasion by Ivan and a coalition of Russian princes in 1329.

What had begun as a local rising had become a full-scale dynastic war, with Uzbeg as puppet-master. Alexander sought refuge with Gediminas, Grand Duke of Lithuania, sending his son Feodor to Uzbeg to obtain pardon. He evidently still hoped to gain the sultan's favor and perhaps supplant Ivan, and initially it seemed that he might do so, for Uzbeg, whose reasons are not entirely clear, restored him to Tver in 1337. The title of Grand Duke

remained with Ivan I.

A modern portrait of Ivan I

Inevitably, war broke out again between Tver and Moscow, with the Golden Horde taking Ivan's side. In 1339, Alexander was brought before Uzbeg in Sarai and executed, but not as his father and grandfather had been. Instead, his body was quartered, which was noteworthy because the Mongols usually avoided execution by spilling blood, especially those of princes. This was because they believed that one who had lost his blood in death could not enjoy the afterlife, and they feared the bloody demise of one of noble birth would bring catastrophe on the *Ulug*. That Uzbeg executed Alexander in so grisly a manner suggests that Uzbeg was declaring that he was no prince, erasing him from history and condemning him to the ultimate punishment. He was further threatening the Rus that they would share Alexander's damnation if they dared to rebel against the Golden Horde.

Uzbeg's manipulation of Russian politics was ruthless, savage, and effective, and the Rus remained incapable of throwing off the Golden Horde, but he unwittingly sowed the seeds of its own destruction. Ivan I of Moscow emerged from the power struggle as the strongest Russian prince, an astonishing achievement for the ruler of a city that was little more than a trading post on the fringes of Russia. He acquired the nickname "Moneybag," on account of his zeal in collecting revenue for his masters from the other Russian princes. In so doing he acquired a great amount of wealth for himself also which he was prepared to lend to his impoverished neighbours. This money could not of course be paid back in full, on top of the contributions due the Golden Horde. Unsurprisingly, those defaulting princes became economically dependent upon Moscow and were in time annexed. Thus, the successors of Ivan expanded their territory and power to such an extent that they could successfully refuse tribute to the Golden Horde in 1480. That event will be discussed further below, but before then, Ivan and Muscovy needed Uzbeg, and Uzbeg needed Muscovy to maintain the subservience of the Rus.

Russia was not the only problem coming from the West. The Grand Duchy of Lithuania, in the 14th century the only remaining state in Europe whose rulers were pagan, was expanding eastward and south into the lands of the Rus. It had designs on the Principality of Galicia-Volhynia, centerd in the north-west of what is now called Ukraine and extending from the borders of Lithuania to the Black Sea. Like the other Russian states, Galicia-Volhynia was subject to the Golden Horde, but it established ties with the Kingdom of Poland and the Teutonic knights against the incursions of Lithuania. It also hoped to be able to challenge the Golden Horde. Uzbeg acted swiftly and decisively, invading Galicia-Volhynia in 1323 and defeating the army of its prince, Leo II. 17 years later, a Polish prince, Boleslav, was placed upon the throne, but a Tatar-Russian army defeated the Poles and penetrated Poland as far as Lublin and Sandomir.

Not long after, Uzbeg died at the age of 59. Probably the greatest ruler of the Golden Horde, he strengthened the internal cohesion of the Horde by imposing Islam, promoting trade, and encouraging the growth of Sarai. Culture and religion – Christianity as well as Islam – flourished during his reign, and the Golden Horde's vassals benefited through political manipulation and pure savagery.

For all his military and political prowess, however, he left an empire with serious weaknesses.

The Decline of the Horde

The Golden Horde was not properly a state, at least not in the sense that 21st century populations would define it. The Golden Horde was more like a tribal collective of nomads who did not assimilate the subject population as the Normans eventually did in England or the Scandinavians in Russia. The Mongols did however merge with the Turkic population of the steppes to become the Tatars. They had much in common with the Cumans, Pechenegs, Kipchaks and other tribal nations, including similar languages, cultures, and lifestyles. Before the mass conversion of the early 14th century, the steppes' tribes also observed similar religious beliefs and practices. However, due to their lifestyle, which required large expanses of pasture, the Tatars never expanded into the urbanized regions of their vassals. Instead, they ruled the lands of the Rus through a combination of political intrigue and terror.

The Russian lands were expansive, and centers of power such as Novgorod and Halych in the western Ukraine (the capital of Galicia–Volhynia) were distant from the steppes upon which tribal warriors relied. For this reason, the dominion of the Golden Horde never really extended beyond Russia and had to resort to constant but short campaigns to keep its neighbors weak. This was the rationale behind the frequent raids into Eastern Europe.

Nomadic cultures tend to be conservative, and the military organization established by Genghis Khan never really adapted to the advances in military discipline and technology that could be found among the states of Eastern Europe. Another weakness lay in the tribal confederation of the Golden Horde itself, in which leadership succession was not governed by primogeniture. Every son of the Khan might lay claim to the vacant throne, and fratricidal disputes were not uncommon. Indeed, Uzbeg's son and immediate successor, Tini, was overthrown by his brother Jani in 1342. Jani in turn was unseated by his son, Berdi, 15 years later.

This political instability coincided with the outbreak of the Black Death in Sarai in 1346, brought from East Asia by trade routes. It depopulated the steppes and severely weakened the Golden Horde, aggravating its instability.

The royal bloodletting continued throughout this time. Berdi was murdered by another brother, Navruz, in 1360. He was followed by two distant descendants of Jochi, but they were also both dead within a year. Between 1357 and 1381, there were no fewer than 25 khans, and none were able to secure the support required to rule.

For the first time since the Mongol invasion more than a hundred years before, Russia was in a position to challenge the Golden Horde. The catastrophic plague did not strike the lands of the Rus until 1351, three years after it ravaged Mediterranean Europe, mostly because there were no direct trade routes between Sarai and the Russian cities. At the time, most of the Russian trade passed from Europe to Novgorod by the Baltic Sea.

Sultan Navruz, in an attempt to strengthen his position against his many rivals and stave off the Russian threat, made the perilous decision of removing the Grand Principate from Ivan II of Muscovy, son of Ivan Kalita, and placing it upon the shoulders of Dimitry, prince of Nizhniy Novgorod (in the Volga region, not to be confused with the Republic of Novgorod). That prince was deposed in 1363 after only three years, whereupon Dimitry of Muscovy seized Vladimir, seat of the Grand Prince, and had himself crowned.

In the meantime, the Grand Duchy of Lithuania, already making inroads into Russia, invaded the land, and in 1362 or 1363, Grand Duke Algirdas decisively defeated a Tatar army of about 20,000 at the Battle of Blue Waters at the Southern Bug River in what is now Ukraine. For the first time, a large Tatar army had been defeated on the field by a European force. The Grand Duchy occupied Kiev, the chief city of the Rus in the south, and gained access to the Black Sea, thus threatening the Golden Horde's trade monopoly.

Dimitry of Muscovy subsequently took advantage of the Golden Horde's perilous position to consolidate his rule and fortify his dominions. The famous fortifications of Moscow, the Kremlin, date to around this time, but when Dimitry encountered opposition, it was not from the Golden Horde or even Nizhniy Novgorod, but from Tver. In 1368, Dimitry invited Mikhail II, son of Alexander to Moscow, dangling the prospect of a reconciliation. Once there, however, he was imprisoned, and he was only released when envoys of the Golden Horde arrived, making clear Dimitry was not ready to take on both the Horde and Tver.

Mikhail fled to Lithuania and requested the help of Algirdas. After his victory at Blue Waters, the Grand Prince was eager to act as kingmaker in Russian affairs, and after arriving with a large army, he laid siege to Moscow. The Kremlin ultimately held, and after three days the Lithuanians were obliged to retreat.

In 1370 Muscovy counter-attacked and Mikhail fled once again, only this time to Sarai. By this time a semblance of order had returned to the Golden Horde, nominally ruled by a series of puppet sultans. The power behind the throne was Mamai (1335 – 1380), a Tatar general and the Viceroy of Crimea. Although he was not of imperial blood, he was the kingmaker and ruled the Horde in all but name for 10 years. He instructed Sultan Abdullah to confer the *yarlyk* of Vladimir-Suzdal on Mikhail who utterly failed to gain the support of the Russian princes. Yet again he fled, and this time toward the Lithuanian capital Vilnius. Mamai certainly would not have wished Lithuania's involvement, but the fact that he was prepared to suffer it probably indicates that the Horde was still in no state to intervene militarily.

Once again the Lithuanian forces could not be stopped, and again they besieged Moscow. Again Algirdas was unequal to the task of taking the Kremlin fortress in which Dimitry had taken refuge. This time Dimitry's allies: Peremyshl, Pronsk and Ryazan all sent troops to relieve the city. Moreover Novgorod, the largest of the Russian principalities, sided with Moscow. Algirdas backed off, and Mamai reluctantly abandoned Tver and placed the crown once more on Dimitry's head.

The relief of Moscow was something of a milestone in the evolution of Russian statehood. The princes had united to exclude not only Lithuania but the Golden Horde from determining their destiny. Still, the Golden Horde had not yet been directly challenged on the field, and for the time being it suited Moscow to continue receiving its authority from Sarai.

Dimitry sought to extend his power over the princes by persuading Alexius, the Bishop of Moscow and Metropolitan (chief bishop) of all Russia to excommunicate all Russians who had supported the invasion of the heathen Lithuanians. Alexius had been tutor to the Russian prince and one of his powerful supporters. In 1372 Algirdas mustered an army to invade Russia again, but this time Dimitry and his allies stopped its advance at Lyubutsk, where a peace treaty was signed. Algirdas agreed to withdraw his support for Mikhail of Tver, whereupon the Prince of Tver acknowledged Dimitry as Grand Prince. Muscovy now undoubtedly held the first place amongst the princes of the Rus.

The Golden Horde had been effectively sidelined in the peace negotiations. Dimitry had not actually declared independence from the Horde, but he acted as if it was no longer a power of significance. Mamai sent an army of 35 000 under Murza (Prince) Bechig to punish Muscovy for its insolence. On August 11, 1378 it met Dimitry and 35 000 at the Vozha River, about 200 kilometres south-east of Moscow. The Rus were arrayed in a bow formation on a hill on one side of the river. The Tatars crossed the river and attempted to outflank their enemy. However, they were repelled, and the subsequent counter-attack forced them into the river where many drowned, including Bechig. This was the first time that the Horde had been defeated in the field and was a momentous sign to all of Russia.

The defeat was also a sign to those within the Golden Horde who resented Mamai's domination. Tokhtamysh, the lesser khan of the Blue Horde (the eastern wing of the Horde, it will be remembered), invaded the western steppes with the intention of overthrowing him. In doing so Tokhtamysh, a direct descendant of Genghis Khan, had the backing of Timur (the famous Tamerlane), who had conquered the lands of the Chagatai. Threatened from both west and east Mamai gambled on crushing the rebellion in Russia and then wheeling east to face Tokhtamysh and the rebellious Tatars. He swiftly negotiated an alliance with Grand Duke Jogaila of Lithuania and razed the city of Ryazan in preparation for an attack on Moscow. He then camped his army on the Don River and waited for his Lithuanian allies. Dimitry assembled his army at Kolmna, near the Oka River, about 130 kilometres south-east of Moscow. The significance of the battle that followed is reflected in the impossible numbers related by contemporary chroniclers: one account records that the Tatars numbered over one million.[15] A more probable number is 30 000,[16] including mercenaries. Likewise, the number of Russian forces has been wildly exaggerated, and Dimitry likely commanded a force similar in size to the Tatar's.[17]

The number of princes that joined Dimitry indicates that there was a wide perception that the Golden Horde was weakening. Beloozero, Dorogobuzh, Kashin, Mologa, Oka, Rostov, Starodub, Vyazama and Yaroslavl all rallied to Dimitry's banner. The only principality that sided with Mamai was Ryazan, and only because it had been forced. A notable absence on the battlefield was Mikhail II of Tver, who, still hoping to supplant Muscovy, probably held back to see who

---

[15] Rybakov, Boris (1998). Памятники Куликовского цикла [*Literary Works of the Kulikovo Cycle*] (in Russian). St. Petersburg: Русско-Балтийский информационный центр БЛИЦ, p.277. 288.
[16] L. Podhorodecki, *Kulikowe Pole 1380*, Warszawa 2008, s. 106
[17] Ibid.

would be victorious.

When Mamai, still at Kolmna, discovered the assembled Russian army, he sent emissaries to Dimitry demanding tribute at a higher rate than agreed by the *yarlik* reluctantly bestowed on the Russian prince. He could not have expected him to agree, and it is likely that he was stalling for time, for the troops of Jogaila and Prince Oleg II of Ryazan had not yet arrived. But the Grand Prince agreed to pay tribute according to the charter of his appointment. It might be asked why, given the solidarity of the Russian princes, he would agree to any tribute at all. The answer lies partly in the fact that though they might defeat Lithuania and the Golden Horde in this battle, they could not conquer them. This consideration, coupled with that of the fickle behaviour of the Russian princes, motivated the Grand Princes of Muscovy to use the Tatars to protect themselves from both the other Russian magnates and the Lithuanians. The power to tax all of Russia also gave Muscovy great wealth and power, as has been stated. It therefore suited Dimitry and his successors to recognise Tatar suzerainty, at least in name. In fact, it would be no exaggeration to say that modern Russia owes its existence to both Muscovy and the Golden Horde.

When the emissaries departed, Dimitry was determined to find Mamai and engage him before Jogaila and Oleg could meet him. On September 6, 1380 the Russians crossed the Don and encountered the Tatars two days later, near the mouth of the Nepryadva River on Kulikovo Field. Dimitry took up a position between thicketed ravines, meaning that the Tatars could not employ their traditional flanking attack. After a series of preliminary skirmishes, the main clash started at about 10.30 am. The fighting was close and tight, given the terrain, and this sorely disadvantaged the Tatars who were best on open plains. Nevertheless, the Tatars pressed forward and it seemed the Russians would rout. At the last moment, however, Dimitry launched a cavalry charge against their flank. The exhausted Tatars collapsed under the assault, routed and pursued for over 50 kilometres.

When Jogaila learned of the defeat he turned back toward Lithuania. Oleg of Ryazan, who had not been present at Kulikovo, turned against the Tatars, picking off retreating units. Mamai escaped, though Mohammad Bolak, his puppet Sultan, perished. The Tatar kingmaker now had little hope of defeating Tokhtamysh. He nevertheless rode to meet him and was vanquished at the Battle of Kalka River. Ironically this was the scene of the first major battle in the invasion of Russia 157 years before. Mamai's fate is not clear. He may have been executed by Tokhtamysh after the battle, or slain by the Genoese inhabitants of Caffa in the Crimea while trying to escape.[18]

Sultan Tokhtamysh briefly unified the princes of the Golden Horde. The ancient division between the Blue Horde and the White Horde was abolished and the new monarch was intent on bringing the insolent Russian princes to heal. Muscovy experienced something of the old power of the Tatars when his troops laid siege to Moscow on August 23, 1382. The siege is notable in being the first recorded incidence of Russians using firearms. Tokhtamysh succeeded in

---

[18] Janet Martin, *Medieval Russia, 980-1584*, (Cambridge University Press, 1995), 237.

persuading some of the princes, notably Dimitry of Suzdal and Vasily of Nizhniy Novgorod, to join in the sacking of Moscow, during which 24 000 people perished. Dimitry's son Vasily had to be surrendered as a hostage to ensure that Dimitry paid tribute to the Sultan-Khan. It was a heavy reminder of the power a unified Horde could muster, but it did not signify a permanent change in Russian politics. It is telling that Tokhtamysh did not destroy Muscovy entirely, nor give the Grand Principate to another Russian ruler, surely evidence that the Horde still needed Muscovy.

In 1383 Tokhtamysh defeated a Lithuanian army at the Battle of Poltava, and although he did not recover all the territories lost at the Battle of Blue Waters, he did in staving off Lithuanian expansion and re-establishing the Horde as the dominant power in the region. He threw this achievement away, however, by the disastrous decision to invade Persia in 1386. When Abu Said, the last Khan of Persia (Ilkhanate) died in 1335, his empire fragmented into a number of Mongol and Turkic principalities. There was no major power to fill the vacuum left by the khans, with the Golden Horde and Chagatai being preoccupied with their own divisions. In the 1360s the Tatar prince Timur the Lame seized Transoxiana and in so doing rent the Chagatai in two. He then invaded Persia. By 1385 he had conquered the eastern portion of the land and was advancing toward Azerbaijan.

Tokhtamysh also wished to expand into Persia. He wished to emulate the Sultan Uzbeg and restore the glory of the Golden Horde. He invaded Persia and plundered Azerbaijan all the way to Tabriz. Timur's support had put Tokhtamysh on the throne and he was furious. He struck at the Golden Horde in Volga Bulgaria, defeating Tokhtamysh at the Battle of the Kondurcha River in 1391. Four years later, on April 15, the Golden Horde was utterly routed at the Terek River in the northern Caucasia following the defection of some of the princes to Timur. The victorious army continued north, razing Sarai to the ground and destroyed all the settlements along the Volga and all the way to Jelets on the Don. Every major trading center of the Golden Horde was annihilated, save the Genoese city of Caffa which was spared. Tokhtamysh escaped the wrath of Timur but not that of his people. The princes deposed him and replaced him with Timur Qutlugh, an ally of Timur the Lame. The real power behind the throne was a Crimean Tatar prince known as Edigu. He had been one of Tokhtamysh's most capable generals but had rebelled against him, carving out a stronghold for himself between the Volga and Ural rivers.

Tokhtamysh now fled to Lithuania and asked for the help of Grand Duke Vytautas, nephew of Algirdas. Vytautas agreed, in exchange for the renunciation of all claims over Ruthenia (Lithuanian Russia – chiefly what is now Ukraine). His power and influence had increased greatly since Poltava. The Grand Duke was Catholic now, and reconciled – temporarily at least – with Muscovy (Vytautas's daughter was married to Vasily I of Moscow). The Grand Duke assembled a great force of Lithuanians, Wallachians, Ruthenians and Moldavians, joined by troops from the Kingdom of Poland, the Teutonic Order and the meagre contribution of Tokhtamysh. He asked for and obtained a blessing for his endeavour from Pope Boniface IX, who declared it a holy crusade, and it must surely have grated upon Tokhtamysh who aspired to be a great Muslim leader.

The allied army plunged into Crimea, the first time a western army had penetrated the Tatar Steppes, and at first encountered little resistance from the ruined and depopulated towns. By 1398 the crusaders had reached the Don, and in the following year it veered west to face a large Tatar force at the Vorskla River, just north of Poltava, the scene of Lithuania's defeat 16 years before.

The Tatar army was led by Timur Qutlugh and Edigu, and they were not ready for battle. In this time chivalric courtesies toward the enemy were not uncommon despite the barbarities of war, and Timur asked for three days to prepare for battle. Vytautas granted this – probably in the belief that no amount of preparation would give his foe the advantage - only to find out the request was a ploy to allow Edigu the time he needed to join his sultan. One may wonder if Tokhtamysh, who knew Timur Qutlugh, urged him not to agree to the request. With 38 000 men Vytautas now faced an army more than twice as large. Still, Vytautas had technology on his side. He planned to construct a field fortification consisting of chained wagons and artillery and the Tatar cavalry would have charged it and been decimated by firepower. It is difficult to see how such a tactic could have failed, but Vytautas fell for the classic Tatar tactic – the feigned charge. As the crusaders pursued what they supposed were routing troops, more appeared from the flanks, seemingly out of nowhere, and surrounded the allied army. Tokhtamysh fled the field while his Christian allies were routed. One might also wonder if Tokhtamysh urged Vytautas not to allow himself to be duped by a feigned retreat.

Vytautas barely escaped while 20 of the 50 princes of his army perished. The Tatar army laid siege to Kiev, which averted destruction by paying a hefty tribute, and Lithuania lost its access to the Black Sea. Tokhtamysh spent his last years as an escapee and an outlaw until he was assassinated in Siberia in 1407 or 1408.

During Edigu's wars, Vasily I, Grand Prince of Moscow, had taken a neutral stance, though he was Vytautas's father-in-law. He was expanding the borders of Muscovy, annexing Nizhniy Novgorod and other minor princedoms. In the preceding century its territory had increased tenfold and Moscow itself had become one of the powerful and prosperous cities of the Rus. The great Republic of Novgorod to its north was still however beyond its grasp, as were the principalities of Ryazan, Rostov, Yaroslavl and the ancient enemy Tver. It nevertheless rivalled Novgorod as the largest Russian state, and Edigu resolved to punish it both for its indifference in the recent war and its failure to exact tribute. The Horde destroyed Muscovite cities and villages in 1408, as it had many times before, a reminder to Vasily of its awful power. Significantly, however, the Kremlin citadel did not succumb, though the environs of Moscow were pillaged and burnt. Yet it was only in 1412 that Vasily agreed to submit to the Golden Horde.

Edigu may have still been able to inflict terror on the vassals of the Golden Horde but these shows of power belied the deep divisions within the Horde. Edigu had taken on Mamai's role as kingmaker and puppet-master, and his domination was deeply resented by the Tatar princes. Like Mamai, Edigu chose sultans who did not have the talent, support or prestige to govern by themselves. The Horde was thus dependent upon the will of the strongest warlord. When Edigu's fourth sultan, Timur, did attempt to assert his independence in 1411, Edigu fled to Central Asia. He was soon replaced however by Jalal al-Din, none other than the son of Tokhtamysh. He reigned less than a year, supplanted by another procession of lacklustre Sultan-khans whose reigns rarely exceeded a year. This time was marked by constant civil war and the Golden Horde began to divide permanently. Sultan Ulugh Mohammad was ousted from the throne in 1436, whereupon he captured the Volga city of Kazan and set up an independent khanate there. Three years later the Crimean Peninsula and the adjoining regions between the Don and the Dnieper split off as the Khanate of Crimea under Haci I Giray. Along the Oka River the Qasim Khanate was established, and by 1466 six independent khanates had emerged. The rump of the Golden Horde continued to control Sarai and a region between Lithuania, Crimea and Muscovy to the west and Kazan and the Khanate of Astrakhan to the east. This remnant is often called the Great Horde to distinguish it from the other khanates, but this essay will continue to refer to it as the Golden Horde.

The Golden Horde had lost control of Crimea and thus of the Genoese trading ports. It thus became dependent on the tribute from Russia, but Muscovy continued to grow in territory, power and prestige. Its ruler, Ivan III, "Gatherer of the Russian Lands," annexed Yaroslavl, Rostov, Vyatka and Tver. Even the great Republic of Novgorod fell to him in 1478. He also reduced the Khanate of Kazan to a state of vassalage. Now ruler of all Rus, Ivan dared to call himself *Tsar*, successor to the last Roman (Byzantine) Emperor, who perished when Constantinople fell to the Ottomans in 1453. The Tatars could no longer strike into Russian and Ruthenian lands and devastate their cities. They could and did however conduct slave raids which had two effects advantageous to the khanates. First, the slave trade – usually with the Ottomans – was a source of wealth and secondly, the raids depopulated the border regions and staved off Russian encroachment into the Steppes. These onslaughts did indeed drain Muscovy of manpower and economic resources for over three centuries, so much so that the Tatars (particularly in Crimea) were referred to as "the vampire that drinks the blood of the Rus."[19] It is estimated that almost 200,000 Russians were abducted in the first 50 years of the 17th century alone.[20]

Despite the power of Muscovy, the Golden Horde was determined to bring Ivan III to heel. Sultan Ahmed made an alliance with Casimir IV of Poland, also Grand Duke of Lithuania, in 1472 and demanded that Ivan pay homage. The tsar refused and in so doing repudiated the 200-year Tatar yoke. Ahmed then mustered a large army and invaded Muscovy. In June of 1480 Ivan sent troops to the Oka (Ugra) River, some 100 kilometres south of Moscow, while the Muscovite

---

[19] Subtelny, Orest (2000). *Ukraine: A History*. University of Toronto Press. pp. 105–106.
[20] Khodarkovsky, Mikhail (2002). *Russia's Steppe Frontier: The Making of a Colonial Empire, 1500-1800*. Indiana University Press, p.22.

court moved to Beloozero in expectation of an onslaught similar to that suffered by the Russian people many times before. Ahmed camped at Vorotynsk on the south bank of the Oka and waited for Casimir and his army, in the meantime mounting raids into the surrounding countryside.

Casimir however was not coming. He would later claim that he was preoccupied with Russia's ally, the Crimean Tatars, though it is probable he had other reasons for not joining Ahmed. Perhaps he hoped that a Tatar defeat would allow Poland to dominate the region. Whatever the reason, Ahmed was faced with a choice: attack by himself and risk annihilation or withdraw with his army intact. On October 6 the sultan made his decision and moved to cross the Oka. But every time he attempted to cross, he was shelled by Russian artillery and the Tatar arrows could not make the distance across the river. Ivan offered to negotiate with Ahmed, but talks were simply a ruse for the tsar to gain reinforcements, a ploy reminiscent of Edigu's deception at the Battle of Vorskla River. For a month each army travelled up and down the river, posturing and following each other's movements. Ahmed found no opportunity to cross and must have been aware that Ivan had had ample time to strengthen the defences of Moscow. He would be able to cross in the winter, when the rivers would ice over, but winter was not the time to fight a major campaign. In deep snow and mud the Tatar horse archers would lose the advantage of mobility and artillery would be almost useless. On November 8, with temperatures already dropping below 0, Ahmed withdrew his forces from the river and headed back toward the Steppes. This curious episode, known often as "The Great Stand on the Oka River," marked the definitive end of the Horde's suzerainty over Russia. The terrible reign of the Tatars ended not with a great battle but with a shrug of the shoulders.

Ahmed was inevitably assassinated in 1481. His sons fought each other for the much-diminished throne of the Sultan-khan and the Horde shattered into a number of minor khanates. The last descendant of Genghis Khan who claimed sovereignty over all the Horde was Sheikh Ahmed, and he was defeated in battle by the Khan of Crimea, Menli I Giray. He devastated so much of the Steppes, slaughtering herds of horses and burning grasslands, that it became uninhabitable. Sarai and much of the region vacated by the Golden Horde was occupied by the Nogai Horde, descendants of Nogai, a 13th century grandson of Jochi, which in turn disintegrated and was conquered by Russia in 1634.

Sarai, one of the greatest cities of the medieval world, was sacked both by the Crimeans and by the Astrakhan Tatars. In 1556 Ivan IV the Terrible reduced it to rubble, and in 1623 a Russian merchant recorded that stone from the ruins was being transported to Astrakhan, by then a Russian city.[21] It appears that Muscovy was determined to wipe the memory of the Golden Horde from history.

---

[21] Н. А. Кузнецова (N. A. Kuznetsova), *Хождение купца Федота Котова в Персию* [Journey of the merchant Fedot Kotov to Persia] (Moscow, U.S.S.R.: 1958), page 30.

The Crimean Khanate survived by becoming a vassal of the Ottoman Empire in 1475 and provided skilled warriors for the Empire's many conquests as well as slaves. Crimean slavers continued to raid Russian and Ruthenian territory, and the last major raid occurred in 1769. But pressure from an ever-expanding Russian Empire and the decline of the Ottoman Empire sent the khanate into decline. The slave trade and the wealth it created diminished. During the Russo-Ottoman War of 1735–1739, Russian troops penetrated the Crimean Peninsula for the first time, and in 1783 the Empress Catherine II annexed the Khanate outright.

The Khanate of Astrakhan was conquered by Russia in 1556; the Khanate of Siberia in 1598. The Khanate of Kazakh, roughly corresponding to the territory occupied by the Blue Horde and the Chagatai Khanate, and the progenitor of modern Kazakhstan, was the last of the Horde successor-states to perish, and for much of the 16th century was the dominant state in Central Asia. In the following century, however, it began to be afflicted by inter-tribal rivalry and the machinations of its neighbors as the Golden Horde had been. It was still powerful enough however to raid Russian lands with impunity. Yet as the Russian Empire expanded further into central Asia in the 19th century with a technologically superior military, the nomadic Kazakh warriors receded. The once terrifying horse archers that Genghis Khan had molded into an indomitable force were no match for artillery and modern musketry. The final Kazakh stronghold fell in 1847, and with that the last Turco-Mongolian state ruled by a direct descendant of Genghis Khan came to an end.

The Emirate of Bukhara in Transoxiana, occupying most of the lands of the present-day Uzbekistan and Tajikistan, represented something of a postscript in the history of the Mongol khanates. The state was established in 1785 by descendants of the Mongols though not of the imperial house. It drew its legitimacy from its Islamism and its ruler took the title emir rather than khan. It continued as an independent state until 1873 when it became a protectorate of the Russian Empire. After the Russian Empire collapsed, the emirate continued until it was conquered by the Bolshevik Red Army in 1920.

The Legacy of the Golden Horde

The Tatar descendants of the Golden Horde continue to live in the steppes, Crimea, Ukraine, Siberia, Caucasus and Central Asia, though in the Slavic lands they have been largely absorbed by the dominant population. The legacy of the Horde remains not only in the culture of the Tatar peoples but in their former subjects, the Russians. The language of the Horde became a court language, even after Muscovy had repudiated the Tatar yoke. Tatar names became fashionable amongst the Muscovite nobility and Vasily II, the very monarch who defied the Horde, was accused of being inordinately fond of everything Tatar. Many Russian families today have names of Tatar origin. Russian princes wore the fur-trimmed cap of their Tatar overlords, and Mongol gowns and trousers were introduced to the nobility. The triangular fur hat often known as the Astrakhan Hat originated in Central Asia and is still worn in Russia today. The Russians adopted the Mongol system of postal communications which created a road network and greatly enhanced trade. The Grand Princes of Russia were obliged to collect dues on behalf of the Sultan-khan and thus a strong treasury and fiscal organisation emerged. Russia adapted the Mongol military hierarchy and created an army of mounted archers to match those of the Tatars.

It would be a mistake however to assume that Mongol society directly and profoundly influenced the Russian. And yet it did so indirectly, by cutting Russia off from the west and thus causing it to turn inward upon itself and develop the distinctly Russian nation and national consciousness that exists today. Ironically the Golden Horde helped to create the very power that would hasten its demise.

In analyzing the decline and extinction of the Horde, it might be observed that the very qualities that enabled it to conquer Russia and threaten Eastern Europe in the 13th century also contributed to its abatement. Mongol society was intensely tribal, giving the Horde a cohesion that allowed it to conquer its more dissentious enemies. Its leadership was confined within the line of Genghis Khan, alone mandated by Heaven to rule the world, and it belonged to the imperial princes to choose who of their number would succeed. This at first minimised the need for divisive dynastic wars, but as the number of Genghis's descendants multiplied, intra-tribal disputes became more and more frequent, destabilising the Horde. Dynastic conflicts are prevalent in most states but they were evident immediately after the death of Batu Khan, the founder of the Golden Horde, in 1255. After the death of Uzbeg, the last real unifying khan, in 1341 they became habitual, so much so that monarchs rarely ruled longer than two years, propped up by whoever was the most powerful Tatar prince. Indeed, it is to be wondered that the Golden Horde lasted as long as it did.

The Mongols were unable to absorb their subject peoples, the exception being the native Turkic nations of the Steppes who shared their nomadic pastoral lifestyle. These could be absorbed readily into existing society structures but this meant that the Golden Horde was confined to the Eurasian Steppes. The conquered peoples beyond the Steppes were reduced to vassalage and retained their own governments and military. The Golden Horde was therefore obliged to expend its energies keeping its vassals subservient by means of terror. As the internal cohesion of the Horde broke down and the Russian principalities became more centralised, this proved an increasingly impossible task. In the end it collapsed simultaneously from within and without. Because of the lack of effective leadership, its once mighty military found itself bested by superior technology, particularly muskets and artillery.

And with that, the Golden Horde passed from history, only to become the stuff of folklore and legend.

Online Resources

Other books about medieval history by Charles River Editors

Other books about the Golden Horde on Amazon

Further Reading

Allsen, Thomas T. (1985). "The Princes of the Left Hand: An Introduction to the History of the Ulus of Ordu in the Thirteenth and Early Fourteenth Centuries". Archivum Eurasiae Medii Aevi. V. Harrassowitz. pp. 5–40. ISBN 978-3-447-08610-3.

Atwood, Christopher Pratt (2004). Encyclopedia of Mongolia and the Mongol Empire. Facts On File. ISBN 978-0-8160-4671-3.

Christian, David (2018), A History of Russia, Central Asia and Mongolia 2, Wiley Blackwell

Damgaard, P. B.; et al. (May 9, 2018). "137 ancient human genomes from across the Eurasian steppes". Nature. Nature Research. 557 (7705): 369–373. doi:10.1038/s41586-018-0094-2. PMID 29743675. Retrieved April 11, 2020.

Frank, Allen J. (2009), Cambridge History of Inner Asia

Forsyth, James (1992), A History of the Peoples of Siberia, Cambridge University Press

Halperin, Charles J. (1986), Russia and the Golden Horde: The Mongol Impact on Medieval Russian History, Carhles J. Halperin

Howorth, Sir Henry Hoyle (1880). History of the Mongols: From the 9th to the 19th Century. New York: Burt Franklin.

Jackson, Peter (2014). The Mongols and the West: 1221-1410. Taylor & Francis. ISBN 978-1-317-87898-8.

Kołodziejczyk, Dariusz (2011). The Crimean Khanate and Poland-Lithuania: International Diplomacy on the European Periphery (15th-18th Century). A Study of Peace Treaties Followed by Annotated Documents. Leiden: Brill. ISBN 978-90-04-19190-7.

Martin, Janet (2007). Medieval Russia, 980-1584. Cambridge University Press. ISBN 978-0-521-85916-5.

Spuler, Bertold (1943). Die Goldene Horde, die Mongolen in Russland, 1223-1502 (in German). O. Harrassowitz.

Vernadsky, George (1953), The Mongols and Russia, Yale University Press

Free Books by Charles River Editors

We have brand new titles available for free most days of the week. To see which of our titles are currently free, click on this link.

Discounted Books by Charles River Editors

We have titles at a discount price of just 99 cents everyday. To see which of our titles are currently 99 cents, click on this link.

Printed in Great Britain
by Amazon